WOMANIST DICTIONARY

Womanist Dictionary

Womanism as a Second Language

BY Thao Chu AND Ngan Vu

RESOURCE *Publications* · Eugene, Oregon

WOMANIST DICTIONARY
Womanism as a Second Language

Resource Publications
An Imprint of Wipf and Stock Publishers
199 W. 8th Ave., Suite 3
Eugene, OR 97401

www.wipfandstock.com

PAPERBACK ISBN: 978-1-5326-8821-8
HARDCOVER ISBN: 978-1-5326-8822-5
EBOOK ISBN: 978-1-5326-8823-2

Manufactured in the U.S.A.   AUGUST 23, 2019

Never have we ever imagined that we would have the opportunity to publish a book and share our product with the community. This would not be possible without Dr. Wolff's support and belief in us. To our extraordinary Christian Ethics professor, Dr. Michelle Wolff, who took the time to contact the publisher and gave us this amazing opportunity. Thank you for being so passionate about bettering the community, teaching us how to love and showing us the importance of caring and being responsible for the community. Thanks to you, we understand that *Womanism* is not just a new concept to learn but the reminder of our roles and responsibilities in every community that we are a part of. It is the encouragement and hope that anyone can hold on to throughout their lives. It gives us strength to redefine our roles in the society, to take on challenges, and to devote our lives for the betterment of those around us. Thank you for being patient with us throughout the editing process. It's our honor to be your students and guided by you.

We could not have completed this book without the support of family and friends. Thank you for making us believe in ourselves. To our beloved parents and siblings, thank you for always supporting and praying for us. Your love lifted us through the journey. To Madison Hoffeditz, thank you for your valuable input and suggestions from the beginning of this project. Your perspectives and contribution means a lot to us! To everyone in Wipf and Stock team, none of this would have been possible without your time and work. We are forever grateful for that. We would like to thank Jim Tedrick specifically for giving us this opportunity, guiding us, and being very patient during the editing process. Your support and guidance means a lot to us.

Our sincere gratitude.

Contents

Preface

The linguistic aspect of *Womanism* offers learners values as does any other social language. While most French learners get a glimpse into the history of Napoleon and many Chinese speakers are familiar with an Asian lifestyle, English non-native speakers like us need to understand the language in a broader scope. Since English is our shared method of communication, we have to adapt to not just one culture, but also variants in accents or vocabularies from multiple English-speaking countries. Similarly, *Womanism* serves the same purpose among the Black community. By speaking *Womanism*, they are able to understand and embrace each other's values and virtues, while making their history known to the rest of the world. As *Womanism* can be participated by both genders, and almost everyone, it has different dialects if observed from various standpoints. Hence, *Womanism* itself is a new language. Language of the Black community. Language of women. Language of men. Language of graciousness. Language of the oppressed. And above all, language of self-love and empathy.

Through the lens of *Womanism*, even the simplest words will be nuanced with deeper meanings. Building a repertoire of more than 160 terms in addition to more than 20 womanist people and their works, our project is designed to help introduce *Womanism* to the society. With this goal in mind, this dictionary was born as a reference for beginners as they set out to study the language.

Introduction

WHY WOMANISM?

As our academic tracks both involve a lot of science, figures, and calculations, we tend to neglect multidisciplinary approach to humanity, history, and social science. Our lack of experience is further exacerbated by having grown up in a rather homogenous culture, of which racial diversity and discrimination are nothing but a mere concept of the foreign land. When we were first introduced to the term *Womanism* in the *Christian Ethics* class, we asked each other the question that most people who are unfamiliar with this new concept would: *How is Womanism different from Feminism;* and, *why do I need to know about Womanism?* Coming from a country where religion, race, and social justice have never been in the curriculum, we were confused, yet curious about this new concept. We know about *Feminism* as a political ideology to establish and achieve social equality of sexes by providing equal rights and opportunities for both men and women. What we didn't know was how closely this social movement is tied primarily to white women. After the first few days of class, *Womanism* stood out to us as the useful solution for this oversight racism. *Womanism* is not taking parts of racism and feminism and putting them together. It is rather a completely transcendental experience that put together the fragmented identities and souls resulted from the multilayered oppression. Because black women's identities, stories, voices, and experiences were dismissed in the society, there was a need to establish their own movement to empower their own people. *Womanism* was then created as a new affirming space fighting for racial, gender, and class equality. *Womanism* focuses on black women but also includes men, plants, and animals. Because of its empowering and inclusive nature, *Womanism* has grown to have an extensive range of definitions. According to Alice Walker's definition, a womanist is "committed to the survival and wholeness of entire people, male and female" and "Loves struggle. Loves the Folk. Loves herself. Regardless."

One of the biggest challenges and concerns we encountered while writing this book was how to deliver the information effectively so that the readers do not only understand *Womanism* but also take initiatives to do justice. Therefore, the goal in writing this book is to bring an easier approach to *Womanism* by explaining the meanings and stories behind its concepts. To understand *Womanism,* we need to first acknowledge the historical racism that is deeply-rooted in *feminism.* Secondly, as we talk about history, we will keep an open mind and learn to understand the experiences through the lens of the minority, the oppressed, the women of color. This book is written from our sincere care and empathy to the underprivileged communities, and we hope all of us, the privileged or the underrepresented, will grow to appreciate and nurture the strength in the solidarity and inclusiveness that *Womanism* foremothers have built.

FROM FEMINISM TO WOMANISM

Feminism is the social movement first appeared in the 1800s to seek equal rights and opportunities for women. First-wave feminism, mainly in Britain and United States, campaigned for women's political rights including the suffrage. After World War II, the second wave of feminism (1960s-1980s) fought for workplace, sexuality, family, and reproductive rights. The third wave (1990s-early 2000s) was when feminism became broader and focused on truly understanding the own definition of *feminism* and what it meant for each woman. Although the fourth wave, which began in 2012, was not as popular, it reached the global audience by utilizing social media and the internet to spread awareness about sexual assault, body positivity, and harassment. The feminism movements were undeniably necessary and have contributed tremendously to the power of women. However, these gender-oriented social movements were developed based on concerns, viewpoints and social issues of primarily white women as black women's opinions were not listened but were assumed to be the same as that of white women. The fact that *feminism* only prioritizes the struggle of white women along with the history of slavery and oppression explained why it was incredibly hard for black women to identify themselves as feminists. Kimberlé Crenshaw, an American civil right advocate, coined the term *intersectionality*- that black women deserve a movement that reaches beyond its gender-specific lens and takes into account their overlapping identities and multi-sources struggles to fully understand the convergence of their oppression. Therefore, history is crucial to womanist methods as it explains and represents the untold stories, the experiences, the struggle and the facts that were ignored for many years. Taking into consideration the social circumstances, we will delve into black persons' literature to analyze their stories while examining the derived womanist methods and its agenda throughout the history to reflect on the importance of wholeness and radical inclusivity.

AFRICANA WOMANISM

Africana Womanism is a unique agenda established by Clenora Hudson-Weems in 1987 that is distinct from White feminism, Black feminism, African feminism, and Womanism of Alice Walker. Hudson-Weems is an English professor at the University of Missouri-Columbia, and during her time at University of Iowa in 1985, she started and maintained the debate that Africana women were not feminists given the natural differences in their history and experiences. Her reasons are that none of these movements could deliver all the meanings she desired, and therefore she coined the term *Africana Womanism*. *"Africana"* names the women ethnicity, their African ancestry, and cultural identity. *"Womanism,"* according to Hudson-Weems, recalls a speech "And Ain't I A Woman" of Sojourner Truth, an African-American militant abolition spokesperson and universal suffragist, in which she debated the accepted idea of a woman through her struggle as an Africana woman. According to Hudson-Weems, "female" can refer to plants and animals while "woman" specifically refers to a woman in a human race, and therefore the term *Womanism* is more appropriate to use. It is important to note that Hudson-Weems' *"Womanism"* is different from that of Alice Walker. In Alice Walker's definition, a womanist is:

> A black feminist or feminist of color . . . who loves other women (sometimes individual men), sexually and/or non-sexually. Appreciates and prefers women's culture . . . Committed to survival and wholeness of entire people, male and female . . . Womanist is to feminist as purple is to lavender.[1]

Alice Walker definition focuses on the women sexuality but doesn't make *feminism* more distinct from the darker skin color of women. Because there was more than just the skin color, the majority of Africana women could not resonate with these movements and rejected to be categorized as feminists. *Feminist* movement was also originally not designed with Africana women in mind as Catherine Clinton, a White feminist said "feminism primarily appealed to educated middle-class White women, rather than Black and White working-class women"[2]. Hudson-Weems refers to *Feminism* as an apartheid, which was said to be dismantled, but in fact, still "masquerading under different guises and exerting the same or even greater level of oppression on the Africana masses"[3]. Therefore, Hudson-Weems felt the responsibility to reclaim Africana women's collective struggles while seeking tangible things

---

1. Harris, "Gift of Virtue, Alice Walker, and Womanist Ethics," 3-4.
2. Hudson-Weems, "Africana Womanism: Reclaiming Ourselves," 24
3. Hudson-Weems, "Africana Womanism: Reclaiming Ourselves," 2.

to maintain their survival. The new agenda focuses on naming and acknowledging the Africana people's struggles regardless of genders because men are not Africana women's enemies as they are to White women. Africana women enemy is the societal oppressing force, and Hudson-Weems hoped to remain Africana women authenticity with the new framework that is suitable for their individual needs.

WOMANISM TIMELINE

1979: Alice Walker first introduced the term Womanism

In the short story "Coming Apart," Alice Walker initially used the term "Womanism," which has developed since into different definitions by other womanists.

Jan 1, 1983: Alice Walker published full definition of Womanism

Alice Walker, an African American novelist, activist, first published the concept of *Womanism* in her 1983 book *In Search of Our Mothers' Gardens: Womanist Prose*. Alice Walker defined *Womanism* as "acting grown up . . . Being grown up . . . Responsible. In charge. Serious," "a woman who loves other women, sexually and/or non-sexually" and the one who "Loves struggle. *Loves* the Folk. Loves herself. *Regardless*." Her insights into *Womanism* have created a strong, welcoming community that allowed women of color to be recognized, valued, empowered and loved. Even though both *Womanism* and feminism fight for the equality of women's rights, *Womanism*'s focus is to reconcile and better all humanity and the Earth itself regardless of race, gender, and class. As Alice Walker said "Womanism is to feminist as purple is to lavender," feminism, a lighter lavender color, did not take into consideration the experiences of black people and their perspectives, and therefore, *Womanism* was created to strengthen the *lavender* color, bringing more visibility to the women of color community, unfolding the untold stories through the new language, and acknowledging the experience of black women.

Jan 22, 1985: Chikwenye Okonjo Ogunyemi interpretation of Womanism through the article "Womanism: The dynamics of the contemporary black female novel in English" and "Africa Woman Palava."

Chikwenye Okonjo Ogunyemi, a Nigerian literary critic, discussed the differences of black women writers from white women writers and how these distinctions are reflected through their writings and novels. According to Ogunyemi, black writers are "womanists" while white writers are "feminists" because they are different in racial, cultural, economic, and political viewpoints as the consequence of historical racism that black writers experienced. These differences also resulted in their distinct interpretation of literature figures.

Feb 7, 1985: The Color Purple movie released

This movie was based on the Pulitzer Prize-winning same name novel of Alice Walker. The story centers around the struggle for faith, love, and survival of Celie, a poor uneducated girl living in the American South, hence reflecting a tragic life African-African women suffer due to classism in American. The movie, however, leaves out the controversial depiction of violence, sexuality, and racism that is crucial to Alice Walker as she portrayed the real abusive, racist, sexist community. Although there were major differences between the movie and the novel, it has successfully reached the larger audience and conveyed Alice Walker's message, emphasizing on the power of having a voice to express yourself, and the power of bonding and empowering women.

1985: Katie G. Cannon published "The Emergence of Black Feminist Consciousness"

Cannon discussed how dominant Christian, feminist, and black liberation theological perspectives were influenced by racist, sexist, and classist ideologies, which was strongly critiqued by women scholars in the social sciences field.

1986: The Color Purple was nominated for eleven Oscar awards

Although the movie did not win any Oscar awards, it successfully delivered Alice Walker's message to the larger audience.

1987: Clenora Hudson-Weems coined the term "Africana Womanism"

Clenora Hudson-Weems, an African-American author, coined the term *Africana Womanism* to empower African women by giving them the authority and control to name and define themselves. She emphasizes race as a primary obstacle that has threatened and put African women through brutal oppression, followed by classism and sexism in order. Africana womanism acknowledges specifically Africana women with their struggles and experiences from ethnicity and cultural background, and it is built on eighteen unique essential components: self-naming, self-definition, family-centeredness, in concert with men, wholeness, role flexibility, adaptability, authenticity, genuine sisterhood, male compatibility, recognition, ambition, nurturer, strength, respect, respect for elders, mothering, spirituality. These tenets are distinguished from *feminism* agenda, which was entitled to only white women, and have become their own framework.

1989: Cheryl J. Sanders critiqued the term "Womanism"

In her essay "Roundtable Discussion: Christian Ethics and Theology in Womanist Perspective," Sanders suggested that Alice Walker's definition lack the aspect of "God-language."

Jan 1, 1993: Womanism appears in American Heritage Dictionary

The dictionary defines *Womanism* as "having or expressing a belief in or respect for women and their talents and abilities beyond the boundaries of race and class" or "one whose beliefs or action are informed by womanist ideals." Having this term in the dictionary shows that the community is moving toward accepting *Womanism* as a separated concept from feminism, and hence recognize its own values.

Jan 1, 1993: "Sister in the Wilderness"—Delores Williams

Dolores Williams offered a new biblical hermeneutic of *Womanism* in her book "Sister in the Wilderness: The Challenge of Womanist God-Talk", in which she used the biblical figure of Hagar, who was Sarah's property and handmaid. Hagar stories resonated with black women's experiences in poverty, slavery, ethnicity, sexual exploitation and exile because she was the first female in the Bible to liberate herself from oppressive power structure. The story of Hagar illustrates the right of ownership that was provided for one class of female (such as Sarah-the slave holder) over another class of female (such as Hagar-the slave) and added to Alice Walker's definition the issue of reproduction and surrogacy. This book not only shows the different perspective of womanists in understanding Hagar's story but also explores the expansion and integration of liberal theology (class), black theology (race), and feminist theology (gender).

2001: Akasha Hull introduced the concept of hybridity in her book "Soul Talk: The New Spirituality of African American Women"

Hybridity is the merging of multiple forms of religions to form a new religious orientation and religion for African people to honor their identities, communities, ancestors, and the Earth in a new land where they were enslaved. Usually the blending between religious African rites that they were holding on in their memories and Christianity or Islam.

Oct 24, 2006: "The Womanist Reader" by Layli Phillips

The Womanist Reader is a compendium that anthologizes the works of the major womanists from the origin of Alice Walker to the present. Phillips systemizes and solidifies the idea of womanism, allowing anyone to explore and integrate the concept from multi-perspectives. This is important as it expands and adds more values the concept of *Womanism* by showing perspectives and criticisms of scholars from all over the world in one book.

Jan 1, 2012: Purple Is to Lavender: Womanism, Resistance, and the Politics of Naming

Dimpal Jain and Caroline Turner explore the politics of naming for non-White faculty in higher education as it relates to womanist theory. Exploring these faculty experiences in shed light on the challenges of identifying and naming in an academic setting.

Jan 21, 2017: Women's March

Women's March was a largest single day worldwide protest happened after the inauguration of Donald Trump because of his statement that was considered offensive toward women.

Mar 22, 2017: Solange Knowles Interview

Solange Knowles, a singer and songwriter, interviewed with Time Magazine stating her pride in black feminism and womanism. As a celebrity and influencer, her support for womanism has spread the idea and concept of *Womanism* to a larger audience, which is significant as it strengthens the place of *Womanism* in the society.

Aug 8, 2018: Katie Canon dies, leaving her legacy behind (Jan 3, 1950—Aug 8, 2018)

Katie Cannon was a first African American woman to be ordained in the United Presbyterian Church in America. She was the foundational voice in womanist theology and created a new branch of theology that brings religion and moral wisdom into daily life of black women. She spent her whole life living her vocation to set black people free spiritually from the white and male dominant views of religion. Katie Cannon passed away but her calling and dedication for black women remains as a voice in womanist theology to value the experiences and insights of black women.

WOMANISM IN SOCIAL MEDIA

When Alice Walker coined the term *Womanism,* the new concept was not validated and widely used as people dismissed her stories and claimed that it does not exist. However, as other womanists resonated with her experience, they developed and nurtured the term to become not only the voice of but also a safe place for women and men. From different interpretations, younger generation womanists have popularized the term into a relatable concept to everyone through social media.

August 2011: Digital Womanist Twitter

@owethumack is a twitter account with more than 3,000 followers created to further familiarize womanism to the social media community. It is the platform for women to empower other women, promoting self-love and well-being.

September 2017: The Womanist Podcast

The Womanist is a podcast for black women with a multicultural identity. It provides a safe space for black women with multicultural identity to represent themselves and truly discuss their experiences. The podcast focuses on current topics and social events regarding relationships, sexuality and well-being.

June 1, 2017: The Millennial Womanism Project

The Millennial Womanism Project was created by Liz S. Alexander and Melanie C. Jones to take further *Womanism'*s foremother commitment to enhance the wellbeing, faith and justice for Black millennial women. Using a unique womanist epistemological and methodological framework, millennial womanism centers the voices of Black women and offers them a space intentionally for doing womanist work in the age of social media.

2

Terms

A

Artist /ˈɑːtist/:

- a term used by Alice Walker to describe black women who were perceived as sexual objects but still lived by their virtues, values, and inner spirit to represent their histories.

Abuse /əˈbjuːs/:

- violence in different forms such as intracommunal, intimate and family abuse. A major oppression problem that is usually not openly discussed in African American family due to the lingering pain, sorrow, and suffering. See *violence*.

Activism /ˈæktɪvɪzəm/:

- the use of womanist methods as a platform to take action against unjust systems of oppression. According to Alice Walker, activism is grounded in her mother's love of beauty and environment.

African cosmology /ˈæfrikən kɑːzˈmɑːlədʒi/ :

- a system of beliefs that explains the structure of the universe that harmonizes to Alice Walker's womanist perspective, which is the interdependent relationship between individuals and the community. Because they are interdependent to each other, the community is responsible for the human's virtues, actions, and vices.

African womanist literary movement /ˈæfrikən ˈwʊmənɪst ˈlɪtəreri ˈmuːvmənt/:

- in order to make African women's lives, struggles, and triumph known to more people, African writers published novels to put their stories out to the literary world and gain the power for their voices.

Accountability /əˌkaʊntəˈbɪləti/:

- the crucial quality for *Good Community,* a value derived from Alice Walker's writing. Being accountable. Refer to the unity of the community, in which everyone contributes to mutual relationality to balance the needs and desires among each other while taking into consideration the relationship with the Earth.

Audacious courage /ɔːˈdeɪʃəs ˈkɜːrɪdʒ/:

- one of the seven womanist virtues that Harris derived from Alice Walker's writing. An intrinsic, often unexpected, sense of braveness that prompts women to take courageous actions. Being able to stand up and take action. In contrast to *cowardliness.*

African Womanist Hermeneutics
/ˈæfrikən ˈwʊmənɪst ˌhɜːrməˈnjuːtɪks/:

- describes an approach taken by womanists towards biblical interpretation, which resembles how African and African American women converse with biblical texts.

Ambivalent sexism /æmˈbɪvələnt ˈseksɪzəm/:

- a double-sided idea that can be understood in two opposite ways. The first meaning reflects the society's disapproval towards women who stood up against traditional gender roles or spoke a language louder than long-standing stigmas, while the other favors and compliments women who conform to social standards with an aim to maintaining gender norms.

Alafia /alafia/:

- refers to the well-being or wholeness of life and community.

Aquinas, Thomas:

- an Italian Dominican friar and a Catholic priest. Known for his writing about theological virtues (faith, hope, love) which suggests that knowledge and wisdom shape moral discourse through communion with God.

Ancestor /ˈænsestər/:

- forefathers and foremothers. In *Womanism*, particularly in African traditions, remembering and honoring one's ancestors and roots to show appreciation to one's inheritance is mandatory. One form of honoring is to record the ancestors' stories.

Appropriation: /əˌproʊpriˈeɪʃn/

- the act of taking something to one's use without either asking for permissions from its owners or making efforts to maintain its original, authentic state. The exchange itself can be disrespectful to the owners because their property, either physical or intangible, is not highly valued.

B

Bible: /ˈbaibl/:

- the sacred scriptures of Christians comprising of the Old Testament and the New Testament. The Bible was interpreted differently by people with power and oppressed black people as they identified themselves with different biblical characters. Black people usually identify themselves with the oppressed.

Biomythography /ˈbaioʊ mɪˈθɑːgrəfi/:

- a purposeful, intentional blend of facts derived from real life stories and an appropriate fictional twist that shed lights on the oppressed' moral struggles.

Black history /blæk ˈhɪstri/:

- voices, experiences, literatures, and stories of African women descent that were considered invalid by the dominant force. Understanding of black history explains the needs of womanism to rescue black people's souls and raise awareness in the community.

Black Panther Party /blæk ˈpænθər ˈpɑːrti/:

- a political organization founded to fight police who used power and violence as a form of dehumanizing African Americans in 1966.

Black women's literature /blæk ˈwɪmɪn ˈlɪtrətʃʊr/:

- or *Black women's writing*, a work that presents black history and serves as a voice for silenced black people. A tool to gain values to and affirm black people's experiences.

Black women /blæk ˈwɪmɪn ˈ/:

- women that were tragically hurt and fragmented from all the oppressing forces but still survived, lived by the womanist virtues, and made ethical actions and decisions. A creative and divine artist.

Black family /blæk ˈfæməli/:

- it's important to know the black family tradition of silence when discussing family histories, emphasizing the degree of impact that the legacy of slavery and oppression had on African American families. Alice Walker devoted her book *The Color Purple* to explain the need of healing and seeking for wholeness in African American communities.

Black church /blæk tʃɜːrtʃ/:

- or *The Negro church*, the Protestant church that has predominantly black congregation established as a safe place for black people not only to worship because they were not allowed to be in the same church with white people after the slavery but also to have freedom in interpreting the bible as they found fit. It is different from African-American denominational churches.

Black feminism /blæk ˈfemənɪzəm/ :

- a movement among black women that criticized feminism based on race, with a widely held belief that sexism, classism, and racism are intricately tangled.

Blue body /bluː ˈbɑːdi/:

- non-bourgeois, sensuous body. Referring to the protests against sexualized stereotype of blackness.

C

Cardinal /ˈkɑːrdɪnl/:

- from *cardinalis, cardo* (Latin) meaning hinge-a part that a door turns. Referring to the fact that all other virtues *hinge* on them.

Cardinal virtues /ˈkɑːrdɪnl ˈvɜːrtʃuː/:

- principles of moral virtues. Composed of four virtues: *justice, temperance, fortitude, prudence.*

Canonical virtue /kəˈnɑːnɪkl ˈvɜːrtʃuː/:

- a set of virtues uncovered by Canon, including *invisible dignity, quiet grace, and unshouted courage.*

Case study /keɪs ˈstʌdi/:

- an observation and analysis of a real-life event that captures an enduring communal concern through the lens of individual stories.

Civil Right Movement /ˈsɪvl raɪt ˈmuːvmənt/:

- a movement led by Martin Luther King Jr. during 1950s to protest against segregation and discrimination. The movement changed the lives of black people by empowering them with validation, self-autonomy, self-love, self-respect, humanity, hopes, and survival.

Classism /ˈklæˌsɪzəm/:

- prejudice or discrimination on the basis of social class.

Cultural production of evil /ˈkʌltʃərəl prəˈdʌkʃn əv ˈiːvɪl/:

- A book by womanist Emilie M. Townes that explores evil as a cultural production and highlights the systematic construction of truncated narratives designed to support and perpetuate structural inequities and forms of social oppression. This interdisciplinary study of dismantling evil as a cultural production seeks to understand the interior material of evil through these narratives.

Critical task /ˈkrɪtɪkl tæsk/:

- An approach to answer epistemological questions by looking at the idea of justice and liberation from the black women's perspectives or conditions.

Communal sufficiency /kəˈmjuːnl səˈfɪʃnsi/:

- one of the values that Harris derived from Alice Walker's writings. A quality of a community being able to build mutual relationships and rely on each other during oppression (racism, sexism, classism) for the growth of the community. Also refer to being resourceful.

Colorblindness /ˈkʌlər blaɪndnəs/ :

- the belief that by treating all individuals equally regardless of their race, culture, or ethnicity, discrimination can be solved.
- *also,* an indirect, mostly unintentional, decision to neglect the diversity in people's experiences, refuse to acknowledge cultural heritage, and invalidate the multi-dimensional ways of thinking.

Compassion /kəmˈpæʃn/:

- one of the seven virtues Harris derived from Alice Walker's writings. A sincere understanding and deep awareness of others' sufferings, which empowers one to take actions to help alleviate it.

Critical engagement /ˈkrɪtɪkl ɪnˈgeɪdʒmənt/:

- one of the four tenets of woman ethics that focuses on the fourth part of Alice Walker's definition of "womanist" according to Stacey Floyd-Thomas. An approach to issues with a curious and skeptical mind so that one can ask constructive questions and grow an idea further by challenging it intellectually.

Credibility / ˌkredə'bɪləti/:

- refer to the trustworthy quality that the community of color, particularly African women, did not have and have been fighting for. In academic discourse, black women knowledge was discounted due to lack of credibility. *See validation.*

D

Divinity /dɪ'vɪnəti/:

- Godliness. The state of being superior to human or sacred.

Diaspora /daɪ'æspərə/:

- the dispersion or spread of people from their homeland.

Diasporic analysis /daɪ'æspərik ə'næləsis/:

- an explanation of the circumstances and conditions under which black women strive to foster inclusivity and freedom for the "survival and wholeness of entire people, male and female." [1]

Dancing mind /'dænsɪŋ maɪnd/:

- Emilie Townes' concept that resembles the way thinkers engage in mind conversations, where their mutual ideas can be intertwined, exchanged and critiqued from an analytical or critical standpoint.

---

1. Walker, "In Search of Our Mothers' Gardens: Womanist Prose."

Descriptive task (of ethical analysis) /dɪˈskrɪptɪv tæsk/:

- the use of empirical research to describe the experience of many oppressed black women.

Dehumanization /ˌdiːˌhjuːmənəˈzeɪʃn/:

- an experimental theme found in Alice Walker's work. According to Alice Walker, any act of negating the intrinsic value and worth or dishonoring the spirit and essence of a human being. Being rejected as human beings. Ripped from the homeland. Often linked to forms of violence and systematic oppression. Resulted in psychological and emotional impact on black women of today.
- signals the ethical implication of humanization and a value of self-love.

Dualism /ˈduːəlɪzəm/:

- the philosophy that the mind and the body are separated. In *Womanism*, referring to the separation of male from female or Earth and matter from spirit.

Devaluation /ˌdiːˌvæljuˈeɪʃn/:

- an experimental theme found in Alice Walker's work. The violence and actions against African women to humiliate and refuse the history and experiences of black people as a results of sexism in the black communities.

Defilement /dɪˈfaɪlmənt/:

- also known as *sin of defilement*, refers to the use of violence of dominant force to abuse the body, mind, and spirit of Africans.

Dignity /ˈdɪgnəti/:

- self-respect. A virtue that is linked to moral justice theologically. Alice Walker refers to *dignity* as a key ethical quality that allows her to find justice and survive healthily regardless of the situations.

Domination /ˌdɑːmɪˈneɪʃn/:

- the capability to be superior, manipulative, and in control of others. In *Womanism*, *domination* is expressed particularly through the power over African women's voices, stories, literatures, and histories.

Descriptive /dɪˈskrɪptɪv/:

- one of the womanist ethics elements that interacts with deconstructive and constructive to analyze the experiences by detailing the stories, circumstances, and moral ideas of Africans.

Deductive analysis /dɪˈdʌktɪv əˈnæləsɪs/:

- a "top-down" approach, analyzing from the general to the more specific. Opposite to *inductive approach.*

Decisionist /dɪˈsɪʒnɪst/:

- an approach to make an ethical decision of what is right or wrong and how to behave according to a person's conduct. Contrast to *virtue ethical approach*, in which ethical standard is measured based on the person's traits and characters.

Deconstructive /ˌdeːkənˈstrʌktɪv/:

- one of various elements of womanist ethics that interact with descriptive and constructive. Refer to the critiques of dominant forms of ethics that dismiss women's experience as a result of multilayered analysis of womanist ethics, which focuses mainly on the theological and religious reflection of women.

E

Erotic Womanist Theology /ɪˈraːtɪk ˈwʊmənɪst θiˈaːlədʒi/ :

- Erotic is not simply sex, but it is a mode relationality through the flesh.

Epistemology /ɪˌpɪstəˈmaːlədʒi/:

- the study that seeks out to understand knowledge beyond its surface level, established on the notion that knowledge must be true and justified.
- composed of two branches: empiricism (true knowledge founded on our own observation, beliefs, and experience) and rationalism (reasons and facts).
- dominant epistemology considers black women's voice and thoughts to be *subjugated knowledge*.

Earth /ɜːrθ/:

- part of the community, the center to which all things are connected.
- refer to the importance of ancestral land and stories.
- sometimes referred to as "n——- of the world" as it also struggles to survive under the system of domination. Valuing the Earth or Earth justice is a central tenet for Walker's ethics.

Education /ˌedʒuˈkeɪʃn/:

- schooling. The process of receiving knowledge. The opportunity that black children were not given because they were set to be in the field. Even if they were fortunate enough to go to school, their classrooms were far less equipped and less books compared to those of White children.

Ethical issue /ˈeθɪkl ˈɪʃuː/:

- a problem or situation that prompts a person or organization to pick a course of actions depending on their perception of what is right and what is wrong.

Ethicist /ˈeθɪcist/:

- a person who is responsible for identifying and recording the patterns, purposes, and strategies used by African-American women to overcome struggles, especially through the development of their plots.

Ecofeminism /ekoˈfemənɪzəm/:

- a movement that incorporates philosophy and politics in order to place the ecology in conversation with feminism. This aims to highlight the parallel struggles of women and nature under social oppressions.

Ecclesial hierarchy /iksəˈlestʃl ˈhaɪərɑːrki/:

- the order in Catholic church, which resulted in limited opportunities for women.

Ecowomanism /ekoˈwʊməˌnizəm/:

- originally coined by Francoise d'Eaubonne, a French writer, in her 1974 essay "Feminism or Death."
- an integrated discipline that revolves around the lives, experiences, and perspectives of women of color to emphasize their contributions to the field of environmental ethics.

F

Faith /feɪθ/:

- one of the theological virtues. The belief in God and his revelation. The obedience to God.

Fortitude /ˈfɔːrtɪtuːd/:

- one of the cardinal virtues. Courage. The ability to confront fear, dangers, and obstacle to stay strong to one's faith and make ethical decisions.

Female genital mutilation /ˈfiːmeɪl ˈdʒenɪtl ˌmjuːtɪˈleɪʃn/:

- a (religious) rite of passage for young African girls to enter womanhood by having their clitoris cut away. Resulted in unpleasant sexual activities, painful and permanent damage to women's vulvas, sometimes lethal.

Fragmentation /ˌfrægmenˈteɪʃn/:

- a sense of separation within the self, mind, and body as a result of racism and white supremacy. Splitting up. Opposite to *wholeness*.
- the origin for the ongoing battle of Africans as they are constantly looking for the sense of "wholeness."

Freedom /ˈfriːdəm/:

- liberation. The control of your bodies, mind, spirit, actions, and decision. Not feeling fragmented or spiritually oppressed.

Frugality /fruˈɡæləti/:

- the quality of being economically with consumption, a dominant virtue that lead to economic success.

Feminism /ˈfemənɪzəm/:

- the ideology that challenges discrimination on the basis of sex and fights for gender equality in all aspects of life. However, the traditional approach was criticized for creating an enclosed circle of only white feminists without considering racial diversity.

Fantastic hegemonic imagination /fænˈtæstɪk ˌhedʒɪˈmɑːnɪk ɪˌmædʒɪˈneɪʃn/:

- an imagined hegemony of white men that makes cultural war on black women by creating stereotypes, reputations that cannot possibly be the responsibility of black women.

G

Global feminism /ˈɡloʊbl ˈfemənɪzəm/:

- a feminist theory closely aligned with post-colonial theory and postcolonial feminism. It concerns itself primarily with the forward movement of women's rights on a global scale.

God-language /ɡɑːd ˈlæŋɡwɪdʒ/:

- Divine language.

Generosity /ˌdʒenəˈrɑːsəti/:

- One of the seven virtues that Harris derived from Alice Walker's writings. A deep willingness to provide help, assistance, time, or resources freely with no expectations for returned favors.

Good community /ɡʊd kəˈmjuːnəti/:

- One of the seven virtues that Harris derived from Alice Walker's writings. A community that serves to constantly promote justice within and outside of itself.

Graciousness /ˈɡreɪʃəsnəs/:

- One of the seven virtues that Harris derived from Alice Walker's writings. An act carried out with good will, tact, and politeness, displaying grace, kindness, and empathy.

H

History /ˈhɪstri/:

- the past of black people. The slavery legacy. The literatures, music, experiences, stories that are valid and truthful.

Heterosexism /ˌhetərəˈseksɪzəm/:

- discrimination against same sex attraction and consider opposite sex attraction to be the only social norm.

Homosexuality /ˌhɒməˌsekʃuˈæləti/:

- the sexual attraction and behavior between same-sex individuals that are usually discriminated in the community. Womanism perspectives, however, value the healthy expression of sexual orientations and identities as a component to achieve the sense of "wholeness."

Hope /hoʊp/:

- one of the theological virtues. The ability to desire and trust in God's promise and plan.

Hybridity /ˈhaɪbrɪditi/:

- The merging of multiple forms of religions to form a new religious orientation and religion for African people to honor their identities, communities, ancestors, and the Earth in a new land where they were enslaved. Usually the blending between religious African rites that they were holding on in their memories and Christianity or Islam.

I

Inclusivity /ɪnˈkluːsɪvəti/:

- the act of involving someone or something into a group or a movement. Refer to the gender inclusivity that fights for both men and women's gender, racial, economic, sexual, environmental justice. Validating black men's voices, lives, and experiences as important and valid. Opposite to exclusivity or separatist, who isolates black men.

Interconnectedness / ˌɪntərkəˈnektɪdnəs/:

- the idea that everything has the internal connection or mutual joint. Refer to the *interconnectedness* between the person and the community, humanity and the creation, the Earth, nature and all the living things.

Interdependence / ˌɪntərdɪˈpendəns/:

- a holy commandment, a key value to build mutuality in relationship. The ability to care and depend on each other for the sake of survival.

Intersectionality /ɪntəsɛkʃəˈnalɪti/:

- coined by Kimberlé Crenshaw, an American civil right advocate, in 1989, referring to the idea that social categories such as race, class and gender are interconnected. Therefore, an individual identity cannot be split. For example, a black woman cannot be a woman *or* a black person but a woman *and* a black person.

Internalized racism /ɪnˈtɜːrnəlaɪz ˈreɪsɪzəm/:

- a phenomenon describing a person in the same or different racial/ethnic groups acting racist toward each other while supporting the dominant idea of the "superior" group. A systematic, structural oppression that affects a community.

Inductive approach /ɪnˈdʌktɪv əˈproʊtʃ/:

- a "bottom-up" approach, from specific, detailed to more general theory. Analyzing the cultural circumstances to delineate the development of ethical or unethical behavior.

Invisiblization /ɪnˈvɪzɪblizeɪʃn/:

- the act of making something disappear or invisible. Refer to the result of the racist ideology that ignores and claims black people's histories, stories, voices, experiences to be unimportant and invalid. Can be expressed in the form of not including African history in the curriculum.

Invisible dignity /ɪnˈvɪzəbl ˈdɪgnəti/:

- According to Harris, "an inner knowing and innate authority that stands in the face of threats of violence against the person sense of self or integrity." [2]

J

Justice /ˈdʒʌstɪs/:

- One of the seven virtues Harris derived from Alice Walker's writings. Balanced fairness to oneself and others, which enables the establishment of equality, freedom, and human and environmental rights. Often relate to *good community*.

K

Knowledge /ˈnɑːlɪdʒ/:

- the facts, expertise, or proficiency gained from observation, experience, learning, and association. See *subjugated knowledge*.

2. Harris, "Gift of Virtue, Alice Walker, and Womanist Ethics," 56.

L

Land /lænd/:

- a property that black people were denied to have ownership. A symbol of the Africans' ancestor and their hard-work. Also, the unequal access to land is reflected through the different writing styles of black and white Southerners as they experienced white privileges.

Lesbianism /ˈlezbiənɪzəm/:

- homosexuality between women. *See homosexuality*

Letting go for the sake of survival:

- one of the values that was uncovered from Alice Walker's mother story. The quality of being able to move on and live with dignity regardless of difficulties, injustice and mistreatments.
- the belief that although racism is vicious, it is not created by God; thus it will be accepted as an evil while values and virtue will be a guidance to moral and ethical actions.

Lord, Audre:

- black feminist who questioned the necessity of the term "womanist" and its distinction from black feminist. Lord believed that the coining of "womanist" refuses to acknowledge the term "black feminist."

Liberation /ˌlɪbəˈreɪʃn/:

- restore one's independence and freedom from limits on thoughts or a period of oppression

Literary tradition /ˈlɪtəreri trəˈdɪʃn/:

- an idea derived from Floyd-Thomas, which states that literature is a valid tool to provide a realistic insight into how ethical values are created and sustained despite constant survival battles.

Liberation theology /ˌlɪbəˈreɪʃn θiˈɑːlədʒi/:

- a religious movement especially among Roman Catholic clergy in Latin America that combines political philosophy usually of a Marxist orientation with a theology of salvation as a liberation from injustice.

M

Moral agency /ˈmɔːrəl ˈeɪdʒənsi/:

- the ability to make ethical actions and decisions based on the virtues and the perception of right and wrong. Because dominant virtues are not compatible with African Americans, womanists derived from their own literatures a set of virtue ethics to guide black people to take ethical actions.

MOVE /muːv/:

- MOVE, which stands for "movement," is a group of African American people (known as radical utopians), who were bombed by police officials in the MOVE massacre in Philadelphia in 1985. The massacre killed at least 11 women and children and destroyed 65 homes in the predominantly African American neighborhood.
- according to Alice Walker, the massacre showed how violence was used to dehumanize black people and exposed the core of racism and classism that measures humanity by wealth.

Moral wisdom /ˈmɔːrəl ˈwɪzdəm/:

- a combination of intelligence with morality gained through experience; the knowledge of being an upright person, helps individuals to act in a moral way when faced with a difficult situation.

Mammy /ˈmæmi/:

- a coerced surrogacy role for black women who work as servants to nurture the entire white family. Resulted in a stereotype of masculinization of black female, the sense of lowered self-esteem and self-worth.

Memory /ˈmeməri/: 16,17

- a recollection of something in the past. In many of Alice Walker's essays, she recalled the slavery time to honor and acknowledge her ancestors who have inspired her writing. Keeping them in *memory* allows Alice Walker to always connect to her roots and heritage.

Mule /mjuːl/:

- as in "mules of the world," referring to the white's perception that black women are sexual objects. Alice Walker's writings go against this idea by calling black women creative artists and intellectuals.

Mutuality /ˌmjuːtʃuˈæləti/:

- (in relationship) a value derived from Alice Walker's work. Depending upon and caring for one another for the sake of keeping members of the community alive and safe from acts of racial violence.

N

Normative judgement /ˈnɔːrmətɪv ˈdʒʌdʒmənt/:

- weighing the pros and cons of moral situations and actions as a means for survival and quality of life.

Nicomachean ethics /ˌnɪkoʊˈmækiən ˈeθɪk/:

- Aristotle's best known work; the theme of the work is a Socratic question previously explored in the works of Plato (Aristotle's friend and teacher) of how men should best live; these works of Aristotle's imply that it was not important to discuss women's virtues.

O

Oppression /əˈpreʃn/:

- prolonged cruel or unjust treatment or control. A form of injustice that occurs when one social group is subordinated while another is privileged. Oppression is maintained by a variety of different mechanisms including social norms, stereotypes and institutional rules.

P

Prudence /ˈpruːdns/:

- one of the four cardinal virtues, meaning the ability to evaluation the situation and make a right judgment and appropriate action.

Paganism /ˈpeɪgənɪzəm/:

- Alice Walker's religious tradition that worships the Earth and Nature as God and the spirit respectively.

Patriarchy /ˈpeɪtriɑːrki/:

- a social system that supports dualism and domination, resulted in men holding power and control over women.

Prophetic voice /prəˈfetɪk vɔɪs/:

- the ideas, words and guidance of God to connect the people to God's will to build a community of faith, partnership, justice, and unity.

Q

Quiet grace /ˈkwaɪət greɪs/:

- one of the canonical virtues. Quiet does not mean unspoken, weak or silence. It refers to the persistence to live by virtue ethics and resolve injustice for survival despite hardships. Grace means being gracious, kind, and compassionate under oppression. An admirable quality of black people under the threats of racism and injustice.

R

Redemptive self-love /rɪˈdemptɪv ˌself ˈlʌv/:

- one of the four tenets of woman ethics that focuses on the third part of Alice Walker's definition of "womanist" according to Stacey Floyd-Thomas. The ability to love one's body despite skin color or being seen as sexual objects.

Resourceful /rɪˈsɔːrsfl/:

- as in *Being resourceful in spite of oppression*. One of the values Harris derived from Alice Walker writing. Refers to the generosity and sharing of others to the community regardless of economic oppression.
- the quality to thrive for the better self and community.
- usually mentioned as to remind the story of Alice Walker's sister, who sent her good-conditioned clothes as a gift to encourage her to survive.
- also refers to the story of Alice Walker's mother, who let her anger starve her family, to emphasize Alice Walker's womanist wisdom in solving the situation.

Racism /ˈreɪsɪzəm/:

- discrimination against one or more races with the belief that the other race is better and more superior.

Radical subjectivity /ˈrædɪkl ˌsʌbdʒekˈtɪvəti/:

- one of the four tenets of woman ethics that focuses on the first part of Alice Walker's definition of "womanist" according to Stacey Floyd-Thomas. The ability to view the situation and make a decision in any circumstances as a responsible woman rather than a victim of racism, sexism or classism.

S

Segregation /ˌsegrɪˈgeɪʃn/:

- the action of setting people apart based on their race, class and gender. Alice Walker experienced the laws of segregation when she was asked to move to the back of the bus, where black people were allowed to sit. Separatism.

Self-love /ˌself ˈlʌv/:

- being able to appreciate and take care of his or herself regardless of external factors or how other people treat him or her.

Self-naming /ˌself neɪmɪŋ/

- the act of identifying and naming oneself with a group that one finds fit and appropriate despite what other people force on one.

Sharecropping /ˈʃerkrɑːpɪŋ/:

- the second phase of slavery, in which black and poor white southerners have to lease land from wealthy white landowners and pay by their free labor.

Silence /ˈsaɪləns/:

- not being able to speak or use one's own voice. A form of oppression and violence that ignores black people's voices, experiences, and stories. Therefore, Alice Walker has their voices heard by exposing the reality of black communities in her book *The Color Purple,* which then faces controversial critique.

Spelman College /spelman ˈkɑːlɪdʒ/:

- an oldest historically black liberal arts college founded on April 11, 1881 to provide higher education for black women. However, the school "old-fashioned" education system monitored students' behaviors, dressing, interacting that even among the black community, women students still didn't have freedom as if they were still under white control.

Spirituality /ˌspɪrɪtʃuˈæləti/:

- a sense of connection to something invisible, and untouchable that can empower and guide one to seek the meaning of life. Connecting themselves to their *spirits,* black people have gained strength to overcome abuses and oppression.

Suffering /ˈsʌfərɪŋ/:

- the state of enduring hardships, abuse, and oppression.

Surrogacy /ˈsɜːrəgəsi/:

- an agreement to get pregnant and give birth for another woman, who will become the parent of the child. Related to black women because they have been known for the surrogate role of mothering. Usually associated with a social-role exploitation, which is best demonstrated through Hagar stories as she filled in various surrogate roles.
- coerced surrogacy during the antebellum period forced black women into roles (usually male roles) that were ordinarily filled by someone else, and they weren't given a choice to refuse as they were postbellum.
- connected to the sacredness of the cross, which symbolizes the dead of Jesus to save humans. However, the role of Jesus and a woman as a surrogate are not compatible or comparable.

Survival /sərˈvaɪvl/:

- the continuation of life or existence as a *whole* despite oppression from the law of segregation or any dominant forces.

Sexism /ˈseksɪzəm/:

- prejudice or discrimination on the basis of sex.

Sapphire /ˈsæfaɪər/:

- the caricature of domineering black women in material culture who is sassy, not subordinate to black men, strong, masculine, against white supremacy and patriarchy.

Self-reliance /ˌself rɪˈlaɪəns/:

- most pronounced virtue in Alice Walker's stories. The ability to rely on one's own efforts and abilities to confront and solve any hard circumstances to protect one's identity, self-perception, self-respect from any dominant forces.

Soft racism /sɔːft ˈreɪsɪzəm/:

- inadvertent and indirect racism through actions or language.

Spiritual wisdom /ˈspɪrɪtʃuəl ˈwɪzdəm/:

- one of the seven virtues Harris derived from Alice Walker's writings, referring to the knowledge and judgement from a connection to Spirit that can guide one's ability to make ethical decisions. Vice: arrogance, foolishness, rejection.

Spirit helpers /ˈspɪrɪt ˈhelpər/:

- the universal energy present in different forms to nurture the black female protagonist on her journey to redemptive self-love.

Spirituals /ˈspɪrɪtʃuəl/: (or the Negro Spiritual or sorrow song):

- a type of religious song to express a yearning for a better life among Black slaves in the American South. It reveals the slave's historical struggle for freedom and survival as well as their worship experiences.

Subjugated knowledge /ˈsʌbdʒugeɪtɪd ˈnɑːlɪdʒ/:

- disqualified knowledge that has been excluded from dominant discourse. Women of color's knowledge was not considered primary knowledge because white people believe that blacks should be on the farm, not in the classroom.

Six Steps to approach an ethical issue according to Harris' readings of Alice Walker:

- Uncover the experience and stories of black people and black women
- Validate the experience and stories
- Ascertain values and moral lessons from critical reflection
- Connect values to wisdom
- Take action upon wisdom and value
- Empowered by these actions to move toward justice

T

Temperance /ˈtempərəns/:

- one of the four cardinal virtues. Self-restraint, self-control, and moderation.

Theological virtues /ˌθiːəˈlɑːdʒɪkl ˈvɜːrtʃuː/:

- refers to faith, hope, and love. Separated from *cardinal virtues* (justice, temperance, fortitude, and prudence).

Theodicy /θɪ'ɒdɪsi/:

- a branch of philosophy attempting to answer the question of why does evil in the form of suffering and oppression coexist with a benevolent God.

Traditional communalism /trə'dɪʃənl 'kɑːmjənəlɪzəm/:

- one of the four tenets of woman ethics that focuses on the second part of Alice Walker's definition of "womanist" according to Stacey Floyd-Thomas. Referring to the ability to be accountable to the success, betterment and *wholeness* of the community regardless of different identities.

Traditional universalism /trə'dɪʃənl ˌjuːnɪ'vɜːrslɪzəm/:

- the notion of blackness in respect to diversity, shades, and gradations.

Truth-teller /truːðz 'telər/:

- the use of language to make concrete and abstract notion of history, while incorporating real-lived experience from our own consciousness.

Tripartite /traɪ'pɑːrtaɪt/:

- refer to the involvement of three parties, which are the body, spirit, and soul in Christian theology. In Womanism context, it refers to the race-class-gender multilayered oppression and the three aspects that womanist authors based on to interrogate and examine the impact of different theological concepts on the social system.

U

Unshouted courage /ʃaʊtɪd ˈkɜːrɪdʒ/:

- according to Harris, "a deep-rooted audacious behavior that walks in spite of fear toward justice."[3] The quality of constancy in the face of oppression, ability to facilitate change under oppressive structures.

V

Virtue ethics /ˈvɜːrtʃuː ˈeθɪk/:

- a trait or quality that is deemed to be morally good and is valued as a foundation of principle and good moral being. Personal virtues are characteristics valued as promoting collective and individual greatness. The opposite of virtue is vice.

Virtue in Alice Walker's literature:

- Generosity (greed)
- Graciousness (unkindness)
- Compassion (arrogance)
- Spiritual wisdom (foolhardiness)
- Audacious courage (cowardice)
- Justice (injustice)
- Good community/good accountability (lack of accountability in community)

Validation /ˌvælɪˈdeɪʃn/:

- the act of recognizing or affirming that something is valid. Women of color's history and knowledge were primarily considered invalid by the dominant.

3. Harris, "Gift of Virtue, Alice Walker, and Womanist Ethics," 56.

Vice /vaɪs/:

- a weakness, immoral activities or immoral traits and characteristics.

Violence /ˈvaɪələns/:

- having abusive action towards another person. Violence was used as a tool to devalue and dehumanize black women's bodies. *Also* used as a tool to regain power.
- violence and abuse are a theme running through *The Color Purple*, truthfully portraying African Americans men (mostly) that use violence against black women to overcome their own frustration of oppression.

Virtues /ˈvɜːrtʃuː/:

- according to Harris, "habitually practiced characteristics of a person or the process of developing good habits of character so that they are a normal part of one's way of being in the world."[4]

Values /ˈvæljuː/:

- a standards and principles used to measure degree of importance or worth.

Value in Alice Walker's literature:

- a person's principles or standards of behavior; one's judgment of what is important in life.
- Good Community
- Mutuality in Relationship: Communal Interdependence

4. Harris, "Gift of Virtue, Alice Walker, and Womanist Ethics," 105.

- Communal Sufficiency
- Being resourceful in spite of oppression
- Being self-reliant
- Letting go for the sake of survival

W

White normativity /waɪt ˈnɔːrmətɪvety/:

- the unconscious social cultural practices, ideas and ideologies that are standardized by the white culture.

Wave /weɪv/:

- a shift in focus or theological perspective, ideological and philosophical ideas that develops into different movements. Also used as a metaphor to characterize the developments in feminism.

White supremacy /waɪt suːˈpreməsi/:

- the systematic belief that considers African less than human but properties. Resulted in racism, dehumanization and fragmentation.

Womanish /ˈwʊmənɪʃ/:

- opposite of girlish. Serious. Responsible. Sensible.

Womanist /ˈwʊmənɪst/:

- a term coined by Alice Walker in early 1980s to express the need for black women to name themselves apart from white feminist ideals and develop a black community that is inclusive of both men and women.

Womanist theological ethics
/ˈwʊmənɪst ˌθiːəˈlɑːdʒɪkl ˈeθɪk/:

- a religious discipline that examines ethical theories based on human agency, action, as well as relationship among humans and nature while critiquing other theological ethics that refuses the histories and *wholeness* or full existence of women experiencing multilayered oppression and social injustice.

Wholeness /ˈhoʊlnəs/:

- being centered in oneself, unbroken or undamaged. Resourceful. Not being hungry. Opposite to *fragmentation* and *splitting*.
- *also* refers to Alice Walker's *sense of wholeness*, which is her attempt to heal the pain from oppressions that significantly affects her self-esteem and self-image.
- the harmonic unity of humanity and creation. The connections of human, culture, and race. Also, the unity of body, mind, and spirit.

Womanist Midrash /ˈwʊmənɪst ˈmɪdraʃ/:

- a book written by Wilda C. Gafney, an in-depth and creative exploration of the well and lesser-known women of the Hebrew Scriptures. Using her own translations, Gafney offers a midrashic interpretation of the biblical text that is rooted in the African American preaching tradition to tell the stories of a variety of female characters, many of whom are often overlooked and nameless.

Womanist Queer Theology /ˈwʊmənɪst kwɪr θiˈɑːlədʒi/:

- according to Pamela Lightsey, the emergent intellectual movement that approaches to explore the impact of oppression against black LGBT women.

Womanist Reciprocity /ˈwʊmənɪst ˌresɪˈprɑːsəti/:

- the practice of exchanging things with others for mutual benefit, especially privileges granted by one to another.

Womanist sociology /ˈwʊmənɪst ˌsoʊsiˈɑːlədʒi/:

- according to Stacey Floyd-Thomas, the study that facilitates three dimensions of ethical analysis: descriptive task, normative judgements, and critical task.

Womanist ethics /ˈwʊmənɪst ˈeθɪk/:

- according to Melanie L. Harris, "a religious discipline that examines ethical theories concerning human agency, action, and relationship while at the same time critiquing theological constructions that negate the wholeness or full existence of women who deal with the realities of social injustice and multilayered oppression."[5]

Womanism /ˈwʊmənɪzəm/:

- a movement among African Americans women religious scholars to fight for black women's wholeness and liberation.

5. Harris, "Gift of Virtue, Alice Walker, and Womanist Ethics," 50.

Womanist /ˈwʊmənɪst/:

- according to Alice Walker:

  A black feminist or feminist of color. From the black folk expression of mothers to female children, "you acting womanish," i.e., like a woman. Usually referring to outrageous, audacious, courageous or willful behavior. Wanting to know more and in greater depth than is considered "good" for one. Interested in grown up doings. Acting grown up. Being grown up. Interchangeable with another black folk expression: "You trying to be grown." Responsible. In charge. Serious.

- Also: A woman who loves other women. Sexually and/or nonsexually. Appreciates and prefers women's culture, women's emotional flexibility (values tears as natural counterbalance of laughter), and women's strength. Sometimes loves individual men, sexually, and/or nonsexually. Committed to survival and wholeness of entire people, male and female. Not a separatist, except periodically, for health. Traditionally a universalist, as in: "Mama, why are we brown, pink, and yellow, and our cousins are white, beige and black?" Ans. "Well, you know the colored race is just like a flower garden, with every color flower represented." Traditionally capable, as in: "Mama, I'm walking to Canada and I'm taking you and a bunch of other slaves with me." Reply: "It wouldn't be the first time."

- Loves music. Loves dance. Loves the moon. Loves the Spirit. Loves love and food and roundness. Loves struggle. Loves the Folk. Loves herself. Regardless.

- Womanist is to feminist as purple is to lavender.[6]

---

6. Harris, "Gift of Virtue, Alice Walker, and Womanist Ethics," 3-4.

Womanist epistemology /ˈwʊmənɪst ɪˌpɪstəˈmɑːlədʒi/:

- alternative ways of producing and validating knowledge such as music, literature, daily conversations, and everyday behavior. Allows black women's knowledge to be validated as authoritative and challenges dominant epistemology.

X

Xenophobia /ˌzenəˈfoʊbiə/:

- fear and hatred of strangers or foreigners or of anything that is strange or foreign. A force of oppression that women of color experience.

Y

Yearn /jɜːrn/:

- to long persistently, wistfully, or sadly; to feel tenderness or compassion. Women of color yearn for wholeness, freedom, validation, and acknowledgment.

Z

Zealous /ˈzeləs/:

- the fervent partisanship for a person, a cause, or an ideal : filled with or characterized by zeal.

3

Womanists and Their Works

Unlike other languages, *Womanism* is spoken through the lens of literary works. The idea is incorporated in the written pieces put forth by contemporary womanists. Since every woman has her own way of looking at life, interpreting events, sharing life lessons, and constructing ideologies, it is worth looking into the works of womanists up to the present day. Learning about their backgrounds, at the same time, will provide a guideline to better understand the significance of their literary journey. With the list below, we hope to delve into history and explore the connection between womanists and literature.

Letter	Author	Works
A	Maya Angelou	I know why the caged bird sings
		The heart of a woman
	Tuzyline Allan	Womanist feminist aesthetics: A comparative review
B	Candice Benbow	The lemonade syllabus
C	Patrica Collins	Fighting Words: Black women and the search for justice

Letter	Author	Works
	M. Shawn Copeland	Enfleshing freedom: Body, race, and being
		The subversive power of love: the vision of Henriette Delille: The Madeleva Lecture in Spirituality
		Uncommon faithfulness: the black catholic experience. With LaReine-Marie Mosely and Albert Raboteau
	Stephanie Crowder	When momma speaks: The bible through African American motherhood
		"Thinking socially" in thinking theologically (Foundations for Learning)
		"The sociology of the Sabbath in the Gospel of Mark" in soundings in cultural criticism: Perspectives on power and Identity in the New Testament
		"The Gospel of Luke" in true to our native land: An African American New Testament Commentary
D	Kelly Brown Douglas	Stand your ground: Black Bodies and the Justice of God
		Black Bodies and the Black Church: A Blues Slant
		What's faith got to do with it? Black bodies/Christian Souls
		Sexuality and the black church: A womanist perspective
		The black Christ
E	Zetta Elliott	Imagining the black female body: Reconciling image in print and visual culture

Letter	Author	Works
F	Maria Franklin	Black Feminist Archaeology
G	Jacquelyn Grant	White women's Christ and black women's Jesus: Feminist Christology and womanist response
	Will Gafney	Womanist Midrash: A reintroduction to the women of the Torah and of the Throne
		Commentary on Nahum, Habakkuk and Zephaniah
		The People's Companion to the Bible
		Daughters of Miriam: Women Prophets in Ancient Israel
		The peoples' Bible
	Cheryl Townsend Gilkes	If it wasn't for the women
H	Melanie Harris	Ecowomanism: African American women and Earth-honoring faiths
		Gifts of virtue, Alice Walker, and womanist ethics
I	Irma McClaurin	Black feminist anthropology: theory, politics, praxis, and poetics
J	Paula J. Giddings	When and where I enter: The impact of black women on race and sex in America
K	Maude White Katz	The black woman: An anthology

Letter	Author	Works
L	Audre Lorde	Sister outsider: Essays and speeches
		Zami: A new spelling of my name
		The collected poem
		The cancer journals
		The black unicorns: Poems
		Uses of the Erotic: The Erotic as power
		The marvelous arithmetics of distance: Poems
M	Layli Phillips Maparyan	The womanist reader: The first quarter century of womanist though
		The womanist idea
		Ain't I a womanist, too? : Third-wave womanist religious thought
		Human tradition in the Civil rights movement
N	Sophia Nelson	Black woman redefined: Dispelling myths and discovering fulfillment in the age of Michelle Obama
		The woman code
O	Chikwenye Okonjo Ogunyemi	Womanism: The dynamics of the contemporary black female novel in English
		Africa woman palava
		Juju fission
P	Melissa V. Harris-Perry	Sister citizen
Q	Chanequa Walker-Barnes	Too heavy a yoke: Black women and the burden of strength

Letter	Author	Works
R	Dorothy Roberts	Killing the black body: Race, reproduction, and the meaning of liberty
		Fatal invention: How science, politics, and big business recreate race in the twenty-first century
		Shattered bonds: the color of child welfare
		The path of faith: Diamonds in the sky
		Sex, Power and Taboo: Gender and HIV in the Caribbean and beyond
S	Beverly Guy-Sheftall	Words of fire: An anthology of African-American feminist thought
		Still brave: the evolution of black women's studies
		Gender talk: The struggle for Women's equality in African American communities
		Bearing witness: Contemporary works by African American women artists

Letter	Author	Works
T	Emilie Townes	Womanist Ethics and the cultural production of evil
		A troubling in my soul: Womanist perspectives on evil and suffering
		In a blaze of glory: Womanist spirituality as social witness
		Embracing the Spirit: Womanist perspectives on hope, salvation, and transformation
		Womanist justice, womanist hope
		Womanist theological ethics: A reader
V	Vanessa K. Valdes	Oshun's Daughters: The search for womanhood in the Americas
W	Clenora Hudson-Weems	Africana womanism: Reclaiming ourselves
	Alice Walker	The third life of Grange Copeland
X	RoXane Gay	Bad Feminist
Y	Angela Y. Davis	Women, Race, and Class
Z	MitZi J Smith	Womanist Sass and Talk Back

Bibliography

Harris, Melanie L. *Gift of Virtue, Alice Walker, and Womanist Ethics.* 1st ed. New York, NY: Palgrave MacMillan, 2010.

Hudson-Weems, Clenora. *Africana Womanism: Reclaiming Ourselves.* S.l: Routledge, 2019.

Walker, Alice. *In Search of Our Mothers' Gardens: Womanist Prose.* Harcourt, 1983.